3-D ABC

A SCULPTURAL ALPHABET

by Bob Raczka

M MILLBROOK PRESS/MINNEAPOLIS

To my my three "B" brothers
(Bill, Brian, and Brad)

Text copyright © 2007 by Bob Raczka

Artwork copyright notices on page 32.

Millbrook Press, Inc.
A division of Lerner Publishing Group, Inc.
241 First Avenue North
Minneapolis, Minnesota 55401 U.S.A.

Website address: www.lernerbooks.com

Library of Congress Cataloging-in-Publication Data

Raczka, Bob.
3-D ABC : a sculptural
alphabet / by Bob Raczka.
p.   cm.
ISBN-13: 978–0–7613–9456–3 (lib. bdg. : alk. paper)
ISBN-10: 0–7613–9456–7 (lib. bdg. : alk. paper)
1. Sculpture—Juvenile literature.
2. Alphabet books—Juvenile literature. I. Title.
NB1143.R33 2007
730—dc22   2005013472

Manufactured in the United States of America
2 3 4 5 6 7 - JR - 12 11 10 09 08 07

A SCULPTURE IS NOT ALWAYS SOMETHING YOU CAN RECOGNIZE. THIS KIND OF SCULPTURE IS CALLED ABSTRACT.

Obus/Alexander Calder/1972
National Gallery of Art, Washington, D.C.

SOMETIMES A
SCULPTURE IS MADE
OF THINGS THAT
ALREADY EXIST.
THIS IS CALLED A
READY-MADE.

BICYCLE WHEEL
MARCEL DUCHAMP/1913
THE VERA AND ARTURO
SCHWARZ COLLECTION OF
DADA AND SURREALIST ART,
THE ISRAEL MUSEUM,
JERUSALEM, ISRAEL

A SCULPTURE MIGHT BE SOMETHING YOU

RECOGNIZE, LIKE A CAR, BUT MADE OUT

OF SOMETHING UNEXPECTED, LIKE WOOD.

YOU ARE DRIVING A VOLVO/JULIAN OPIE/1996
LISSON GALLERY, LONDON, ENGLAND

ALL SCULPTURES ARE THREE-DIMENSIONAL. MOST CAN BE LOOKED AT FROM ALL SIDES.

TANGO/ELIE
NADELMAN/ CA. 1920–1924
WHITNEY MUSEUM OF
AMERICAN ART,
NEW YORK, NEW YORK

E

THIS SCULPTURE CAN BE
LOOKED AT FROM JUST ONE
SIDE. IT'S CALLED A RELIEF.

CARVED AMERICAN EAGLE
JOHN BELLAMY/1880
HYLAND GRANBY ANTIQUES,
HYANNIS PORT,
MASSACHUSETTS

F is for Family

SOME SCULPTURES ARE

AT HOME OUTDOORS.

FAMILY GROUP
HENRY MOORE
1948–1949
HENRY MOORE
FOUNDATION,
PERRY GREEN,
HERTFORDSHIRE,
ENGLAND

SOME OUTDOOR
SCULPTURES ARE SO
BIG, YOU CAN WALK
RIGHT UNDER THEM.
OR THEY CAN WALK
RIGHT OVER YOU.

WALKING MAN/JONATHAN BOROFSKY/1994–1995
MUNICH RE HEADQUARTERS, MUNICH, GERMANY

H is for Horse

A SCULPTURE CAN BE
PIECES OF SCRAP METAL
THAT THE SCULPTOR
FINDS AND FORMS INTO
A FAMILIAR-LOOKING
SHAPE . . .

Ikezuke/Deborah Butterfield/1994
Greg Kucera Gallery, Seattle, Washington

I is for Instrument

. . . OR

A FAMILIAR-SOUNDING SHAPE.

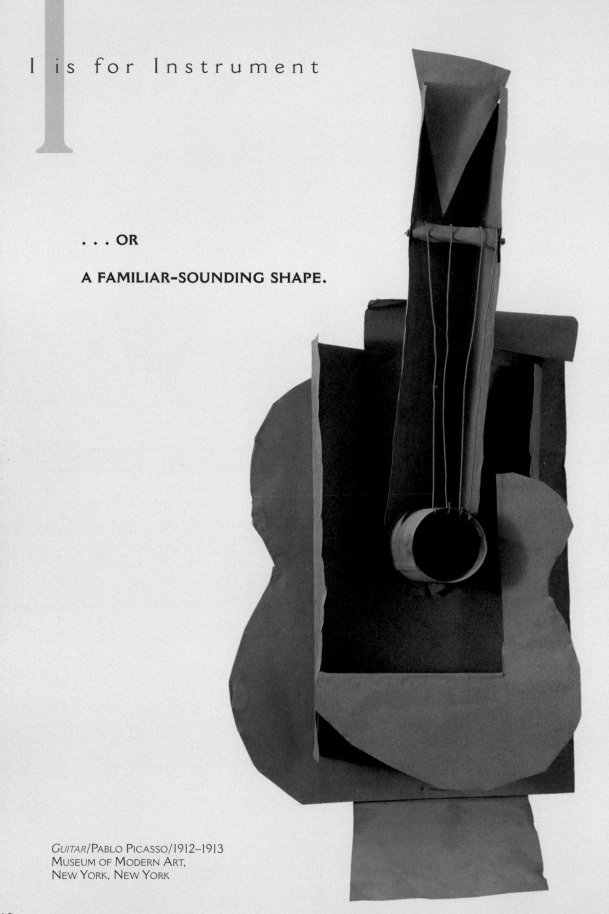

Guitar/Pablo Picasso/1912–1913
Museum of Modern Art,
New York, New York

J is for Junk

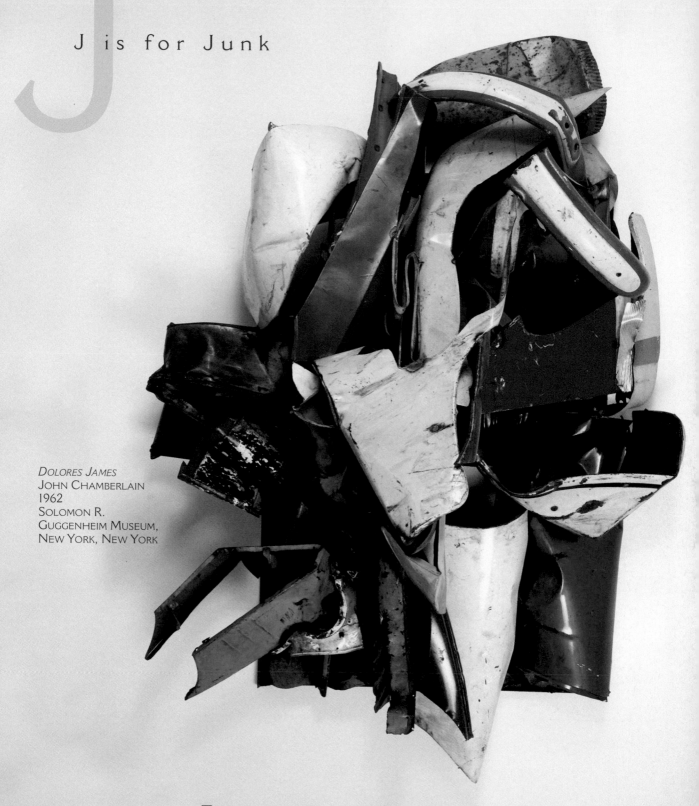

Dolores James
John Chamberlain
1962
Solomon R.
Guggenheim Museum,
New York, New York

EVEN THE PIECES OF SOMETHING THAT WAS WRECKED CAN BE TURNED INTO A SCULPTURE.

SOMETIMES, TWO COMPLETELY DIFFERENT SCULPTURES . . .

THE KISS/CONSTANTIN BRANCUSI/1908–1909, PRIVATE COLLECTION

LOVE
ROBERT INDIANA/1966
BRIGHAM YOUNG UNIVERSITY
MUSEUM OF ART, PROVO,
UTAH

. . . CAN SAY EXACTLY THE SAME THING.

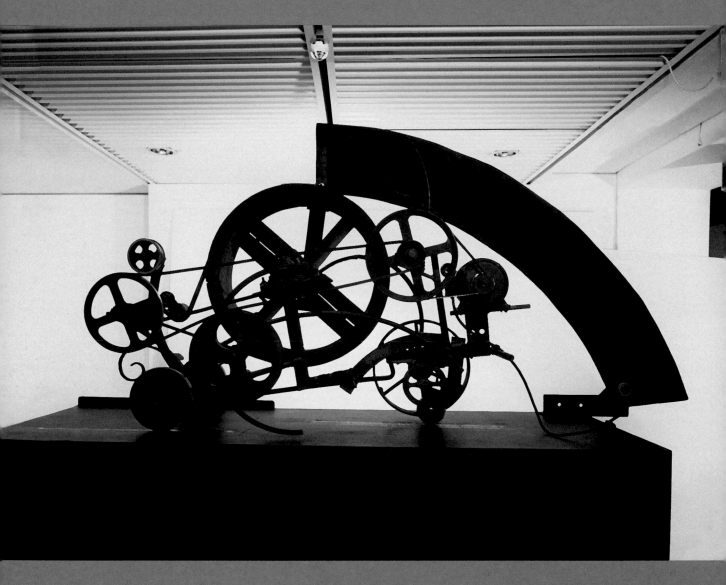

A SCULPTURE CAN HAVE MOVING PARTS.

THIS IS CALLED KINETIC SCULPTURE.

CHARIOT MK IV/JEAN TINGUELY/1966
MODERNA MUSEET, STOCKHOLM, SWEDEN

OR A

SCULPTURE

CAN HAVE

ONE PART

THAT STANDS

OUT.

Nose
ALBERTO GIACOMETTI
1947
SOLOMON R. GUGGENHEIM MUSEUM,
NEW YORK, NEW YORK

O is for Obelisk

P is for Pyramid

SOME SCULPTURES LOOK IMPOSSIBLE.

18

Broken Obelisk
Barnett
Newman
1963–1967
Rothko
Chapel,
Houston,
Texas

19

Q is for Quarrel

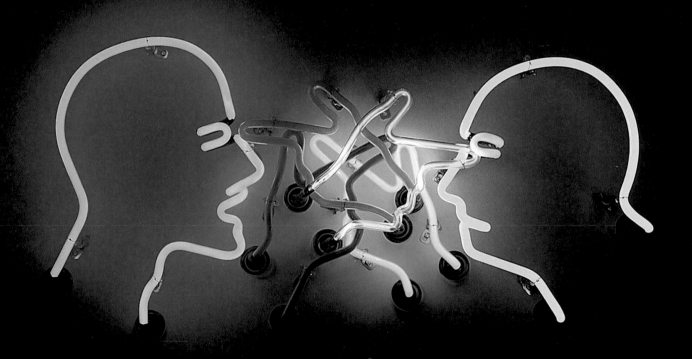

A SCULPTURE CAN BE MADE OUT OF LIGHT.

DOUBLE POKE IN THE EYE II/BRUCE NAUMAN/1985
KEMPER MUSEUM OF CONTEMPORARY ART, KANSAS CITY, MISSOURI

OR IT CAN MAKE YOU SEE

SOMETHING THAT ISN'T THERE.

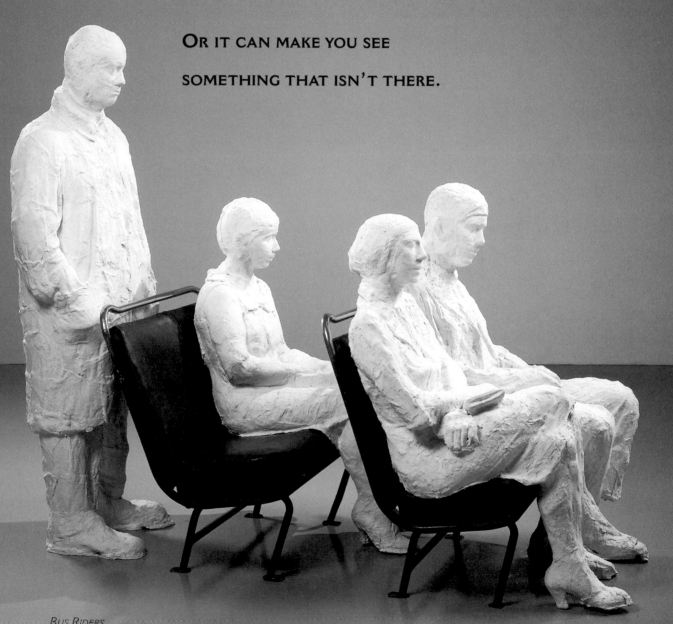

BUS RIDERS
GEORGE SEGAL/1964
HIRSHHORN MUSEUM AND SCULPTURE GARDEN,
WASHINGTON, D.C.

S is for Spoon

A SCULPTURE CAN MAKE YOU SMILE

Spoonbridge and Cherry/Claes Oldenburg
and Coosje van Bruggen/1985–1988
Walker Art Center, Minneapolis, Minnesota

T is for Tablecloth

OR MAKE YOU THINK

ABOUT DINNER.

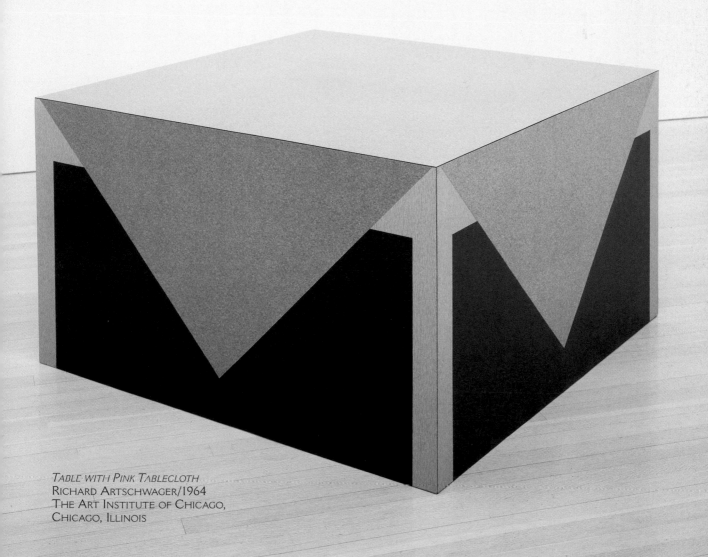

TABLE WITH PINK TABLECLOTH
RICHARD ARTSCHWAGER/1964
THE ART INSTITUTE OF CHICAGO,
CHICAGO, ILLINOIS

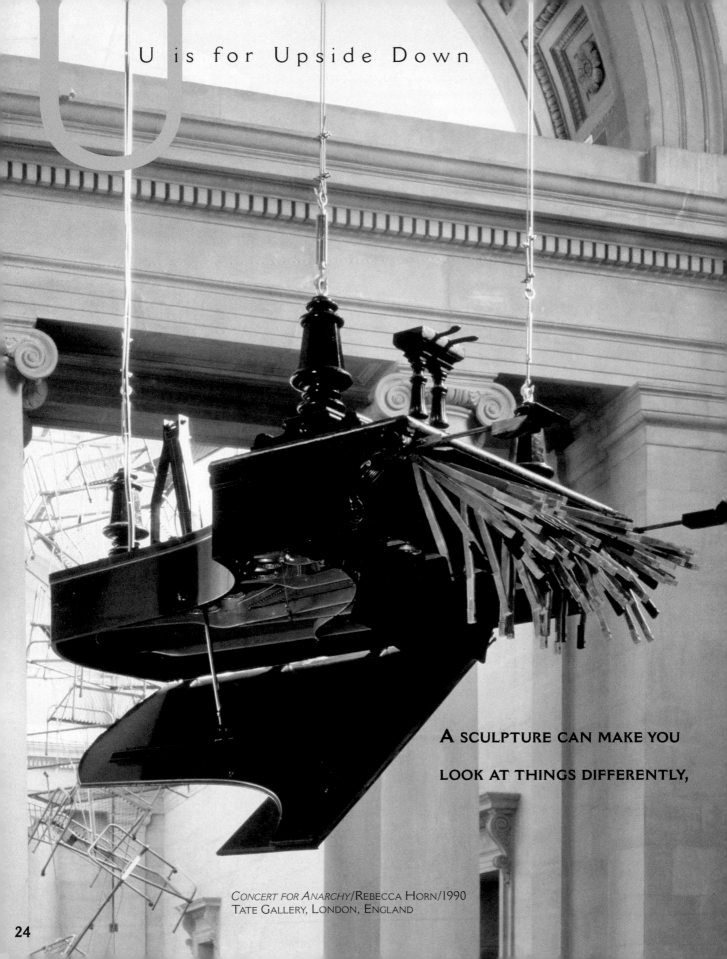

U is for Upside Down

A SCULPTURE CAN MAKE YOU LOOK AT THINGS DIFFERENTLY,

CONCERT FOR ANARCHY/REBECCA HORN/1990
TATE GALLERY, LONDON, ENGLAND

EVEN THINGS YOU SEE EVERY DAY.

New Hoover Celebrity III / Jeff Koons / 1980
Museum of Contemporary Art, Los Angeles, California

A Case for an Angel II
Antony Gormley
1990
Contemporary Sculpture Center
Tokyo, Japan

W is for Wings

A SCULPTURE CAN

HELP YOUR

IMAGINATION SOAR.

A SCULPTURE CAN MEAN DIFFERENT THINGS TO DIFFERENT PEOPLE,

THE X
RONALD BLADEN/1967
MIAMI-DADE ART IN
PUBLIC PLACES,
MIAMI, FLORIDA

Y is for Yellow

OR IT CAN MEAN DIFFERENT THINGS TO THE SAME PERSON ON DIFFERENT DAYS,

MIDDAY/ANTHONY CARO/1960
MUSEUM OF MODERN ART,
NEW YORK, NEW YORK

BECAUSE THE

MORE YOU

LOOK AT A

SCULPTURE,

THE MORE

YOU SEE.

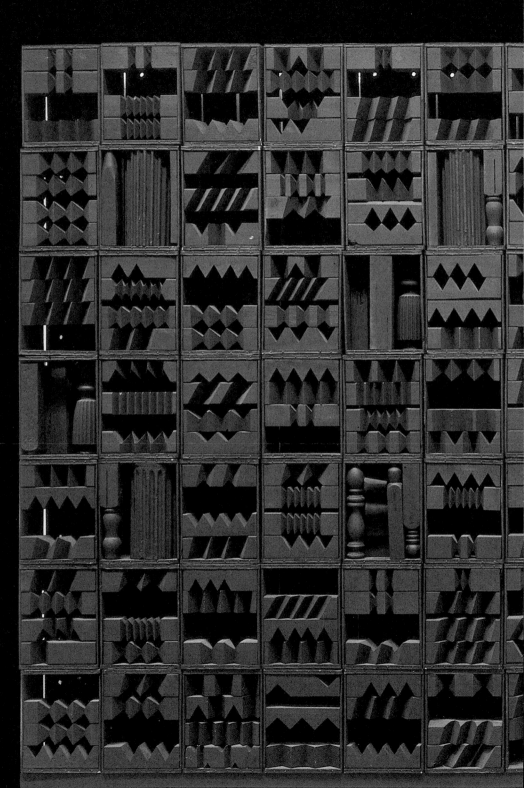

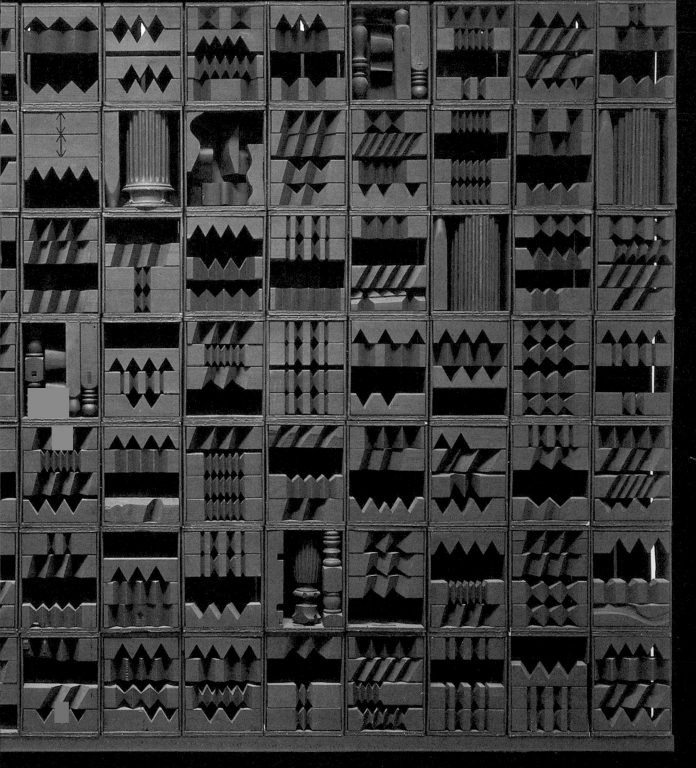

Luminous Zag: Night/Louise Nevelson/1971
Solomon R. Guggenheim Museum, New York, New York

Cover art courtesy of: Claes Oldenburg and Coosje van Bruggen, *Spoonbridge and Cherry*, 1985–1988, aluminum, stainless steel, paint, 354 x 618 x 162" overall. Collection Walker Art Center, Minneapolis. Gift of Frederick R. Weisman in honor of his parents, William and Mary Weisman, 1988. © Claes Oldenburg and Coosje van Bruggen. *Interior art courtesy of: **Page 3:** Alexander Calder, *Obus*, 1972, painted sheet metal, 3.618 x 2.276 x 152 x 89 5/8). Collection of Mr. and Mrs. Paul Mellon. Image © Board of Trustees, National Gallery of Art, Washington. © 2005 Estate of Alexander Calder / Artists Rights Society (ARS), New York. **Page 4:** Marcel Duchamp (Blainville, France, 1887– Neuilly sur Seine, 1968), *Bicycle Wheel*, 1913/1964, assisted readymade: bicycle wheel and fork mounted on white stool, I/II, 126.5 x 63.5 x 31.8. The Vera, Silvia and Arturo Schwarz Collection of Dada and Surrealist Art; Collection Israel Museum, Jerusalem. Photo courtesy of © Israel Museum, Jerusalem/Avshalom Avital.© 2005 Artists Rights Society (ARS), New York / ADAGP, Paris / Succession Marcel Duchamp. **Page 5:** Courtesy of Lisson Gallery and Julian Opie. **Page 6:** Elie Nadelman (1882–1946), *Tango*, ca.1920–1924, painted cherry wood and gesso, overall: 35 7/8 x 26 x 13 7/8 in. (91.1 x 66 x 35.2 cm). Whitney Museum of American Art, New York; Purchase, with funds from the Mr. and Mrs. Arthur G. Altschul Purchase Fund, the Joan and Lester Avnet Purchase Fund, the Edgar William and Bernice Chrysler Garbisch Purchase Fund, the Mrs. Robert C. Graham Purchase Fund in honor of John I. H. Baur, the Mrs. Percy Uris Purchase Fund and the Henry Schnakenberg Purchase Fund in honor of Juliana Force 88.1a-c. **Page 7:** Photo courtesy of Hyland Granby Antiques, Hyannis MA. **Page 8:** The work reproduced by permission of the Henry Moore Foundation. Photo by Anita Feldman Bennet. **Page 9:** Jonathan Borofsky, *Walking Man*, 1994-95, fiberglass hand shaped over steel, 56' x 57'6" x 19'8". Courtesy of the Paula Cooper Gallery, New York. **Pages 10-11:** Deborah Buck-Butterfield, *Ikezuke*, 1994, found steel, welded, 84 x 103 x 36 inches. Photo courtesy of the artist. **Page 12:** © The Museum of Modern Art / Licensed by SCALA / Art Resources, NY. © 2005 Estate of Pablo Picasso / Artists Rights Society (ARS), New York. **Page 13:** John Chamberlain, *Dolores James*, 1962, welded and painted steel, 76 x 97 x 39 inches (193 x 246.4 x 99.1 cm). Solomon R. Guggenheim Museum, New York. 70.1925. Photograph by David Heald © The Salomon R. Guggenheim Foundation, New York. © 2005 John Chamberlain / Artists Rights Society (ARS), New York. **Page 14:** *The Kiss*, 1908–1909 (plaster) by Brancusi, Constantin (1876–1957); Private Collection/Christie's Images/Bridgeman Art Library. © 2005 Artists Rights Society (ARS), New York / ADAGP, Paris. **Page 15:** © 2005 Morgan Art Foundation Ltd. / Artists Rights Society (ARS), New York. Photo courtesy of

Brigham Young University Museum of Art. All Rights Reserved. **Page 16:** Jean Tinguely, *Chariot MK IV*, 1966, 210 x 106 x 65 cm, painted iron, wood, motor. Collection of Moderna Museet, Stockholm. (Photo courtesy of Moderna Museet, Stockholm). © 2005 Artists Rights Society (ARS), New York / ADAGP, Paris. **Page 17:** Alberto Giacometti, *Nose (Le Nez)*, 1947, cast 1965, bronze, wire, rope & steel; 31 7/8 x 38 3/8 x 15 1/2 inches (81 x 97.5 x 39.4 cm) overall. Solomon R. Guggenheim Museum, New York. 66.1807. Photograph by David Heald © The Salomon R. Guggenheim Foundation, New York. © 2005 Artists Rights Society (ARS), New York / ADAGP, Paris. **Pages 18-19:** View of The Rothko Chapel showing the *Broken Obelisk* by Barnett Newman (1967), dedicated to the Rev. Martin Luther King, Jr. Photo by Hickey-Robertson. © 2005 Barnett Newman Foundation / Artists Rights Society (ARS), New York. **Page 20:** Collection of the Kemper Museum of Contemporary Art, Kansas City, MO; Bebe and Crosby Kemper Collection, Gift of the R.C.Kemper Charitable Trust and Foundation, 1995.54. © 2005 Bruce Nauman / Artists Rights Society (ARS), New York. **Page 21:** Hirshhorn Museum and Sculpture Garden, Smithsonian Institution. Gift of Joseph H. Hirshhorn, 1966. Photograph by Lee Stalsworth. **Page 22:** Claes Oldenburg and Coosje van Bruggen, *Spoonbridge and Cherry*, 1985-1988, aluminum, stainless steel, paint, 354 x 618 x 162" overall. Collection Walker Art Center, Minneapolis. Gift of Frederick R. Weisman in honor of his parents, William and Mary Weisman, 1988. © Claes Oldenburg and Coosje van Bruggen. **Page 23:** Richard Artschwager, American, b.1924, *Table with Pink Tablecloth*, 1964, formica on wood, 64.8 x 111.8 x 111.8 cm, Gift of Lannan Foundation, 1997.133 in situ against light background. Photograph by Susan Einstein. Reproduction: The Art Institute of Chicago. © 2005 Richard Artschwager / Artists Rights Society (ARS), New York. **Page 24:** © 2005 Tate Gallery, London / Art Resource, NY. © 2005 Artists Rights Society (ARS), New York / VG Bild-Kunst, Bonn. **Page 25:** Jeff Koons, *New Hoover Celebrity III*, 1980, Vacuum cleaner, plexiglass tubes, and fluorescent lights, 11" x 20" x 38". © Jeff Koons. The Museum of Contemporary Art, Los Angeles. Gift of Lannan Foundation. **Pages 26-27:** © Courtesy of the artist and Jay Jopling / White Cube. **Page 28:** Courtesy of Miami-Dade Art in Public Places. Photo by Brandi Reddick. **Page 29:** © Sir Anthony Caro / Barford Sculptures Ltd. © The Museum of Modern Art / Licensed by SCALA / Art Resource, NY. **Pages 30-31:** Louise Nevelson, *Luminous Zag: Night*, 1971, painted wood (105 boxes), 120 x 193 x 10 3/4 inches (304.8 x 490.3 x 27.3 cm) overall. Solomon R. Guggenheim Museum, New York. Gift, Mr. and Mrs. Sidney Singer, 1977. 77.2325. Photograph by David Heald © The Solomon R. Guggenheim Foundation, New York. © 2005 Estate of Louise Nevelson / Artists Rights Society (ARS), New York.